YOU ARE BRAVE!

D0062279

ENTER AT YOUR OWN RISK!

DUDE VAULT!

OPEN IT UP MAKE STUFF UP
SEE IN 3D!

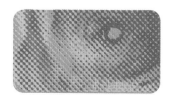

3D
SPECS

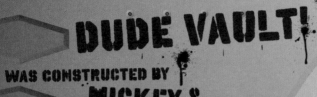

DUDE VAULT!

WAS CONSTRUCTED BY
MICKEY &
CHERYL GILL

WHO WERE SUBSEQUENTLY
PLACED IN TOTAL
LOCK-DOWN IN ITS FAR
RECESSES BY
OCTO-ALIEN
INTELLIGENCE!

help

FINE print
PUBLISHING

Fine Print Publishing Company
P.O. Box 916401
Longwood, Florida 32791-6401

Created in the U.S.A. & Printed in China
This book is printed on acid-free paper.

978-1-892951-69-4

2 3 5 7 9 10 8 6 4 1

thedudebook.com

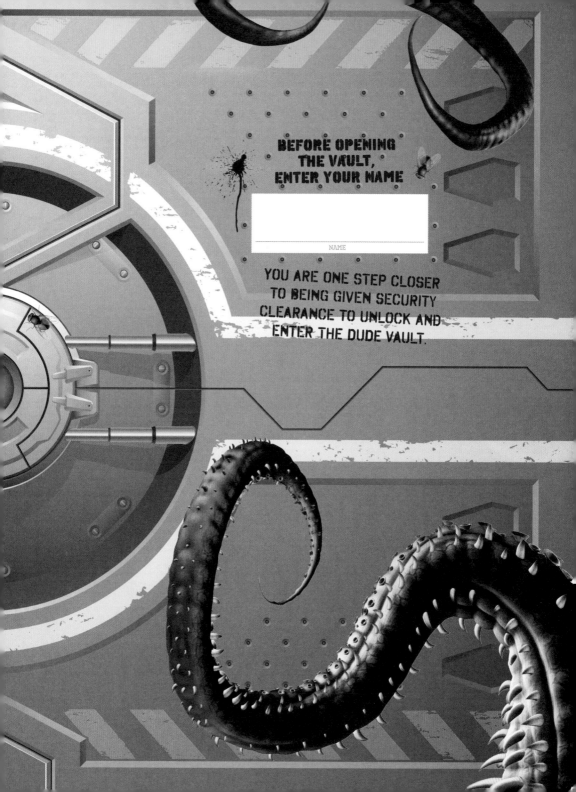

BEFORE OPENING
THE VAULT,
ENTER YOUR NAME

NAME

YOU ARE ONE STEP CLOSER
TO BEING GIVEN SECURITY
CLEARANCE TO UNLOCK AND
ENTER THE DUDE VAULT.

WITH **3D** TECHNOLOGY
THE **DUDE VAULT!**
HOUSES SECRET INFORMATION AND IDEAS
THAT COULD CHANGE LIFE AS

BROS KNOW IT.

TAG AND LABEL A NEW SPECIES OF MONSTER.

CREATE A SUPERHERO OR VILLAIN FROM
WHAT A DOG LEAVES BEHIND.

CONTROL THE PIPING
HOT CONTENTS OF A
SPEW-INDUCING VOLCANO.

INVENT AN
OUTRAGEOUSLY
DISGUSTING SMELL GEL.

IT'S ALL IN A DAY'S WORK
ONCE YOU GAIN ACCESS TO
THE VAULT.

FOR MAXIMUM VIEWING IMPACT
WEAR YOUR 3D GLASSES TO LOOK
AT PAGES THAT HAVE THE 3D
DUDE ON THEM.

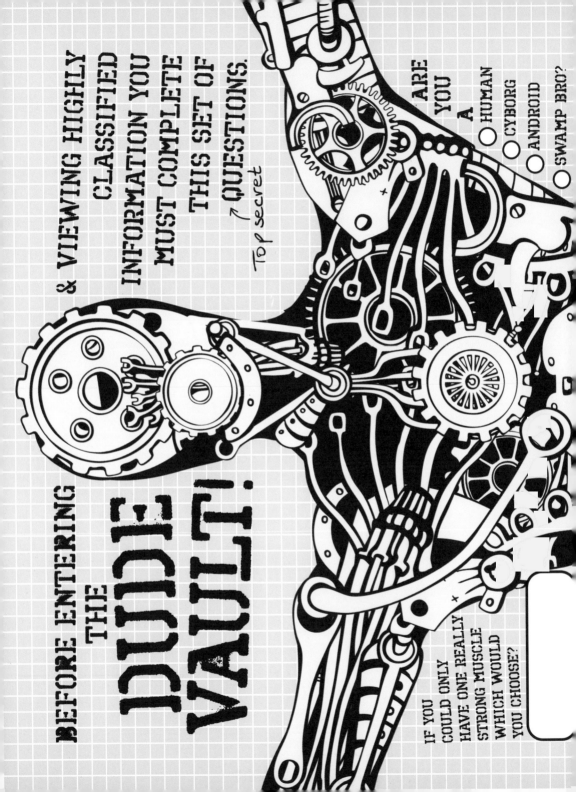

BEFORE ENTERING THE **DUDE VAULT!**

& VIEWING HIGHLY CLASSIFIED INFORMATION YOU MUST COMPLETE THIS SET OF 7 QUESTIONS.

Top secret

ARE YOU A

○ HUMAN
○ CYBORG
○ ANDROID
○ SWAMP BRO?

IF YOU COULD ONLY HAVE ONE REALLY STRONG MUSCLE WHICH WOULD YOU CHOOSE?

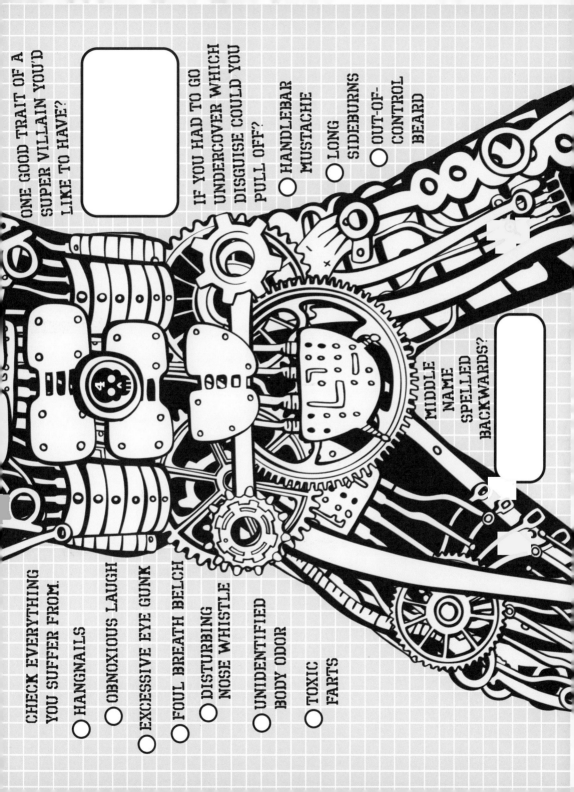

ONE GOOD TRAIT OF A SUPER VILLAIN YOU'D LIKE TO HAVE?

IF YOU HAD TO GO UNDERCOVER WHICH DISGUISE COULD YOU PULL OFF?

- HANDLEBAR MUSTACHE
- LONG SIDEBURNS
- OUT-OF-CONTROL BEARD

MIDDLE NAME SPELLED BACKWARDS?

CHECK EVERYTHING YOU SUFFER FROM.

- HANGNAILS
- OBNOXIOUS LAUGH
- EXCESSIVE EYE GUNK
- FOUL BREATH BELCH
- DISTURBING NOSE WHISTLE
- UNIDENTIFIED BODY ODOR
- TOXIC FARTS

SECRET AGENT MAN CODE NAMES

THE DUDE VAULT CONTAINS VERY SENSITIVE MATERIAL. YOU'LL NEED A CODE NAME, AND YOU'LL NEED TO CHANGE IT A LOT ... TO KEEP EVIL SPIES OFF YOUR TRAIL.

1. COMBINE SOME OF THESE WORDS TO CREATE COOL CODE NAMES.

NINJA	HIDDEN	NIGHT CRAWLER	MISTER
FLYING	COBRA	INVISIBLE	SPIDER
CORN NUTS	MACE	WAFFLE FRIES	CHEESE DOODLE
MASTER	DOCTOR	SCORPION	RED
DRAGON	FIRE	SLEDGE	KING

2. LOG IN THE DATE, TIME, AND A NEW CODE NAME EACH TIME YOU ENTER THE VAULT.

DATE/TIME	CODE NAME

DATE/TIME	CODE NAME

DATE/TIME	CODE NAME

DATE/TIME	CODE NAME

DATE/TIME	CODE NAME

DATE/TIME	CODE NAME

DATE/TIME	CODE NAME

DATE/TIME	CODE NAME

I'VE GOT MY EYE ON YOU

SEE IT IN 3D

3D DUDE

SYMBOLS ARE HIDDEN ON THE PAGES OF **DUDE VAULT!** FIND THEM AND GAIN ACCESS TO MORE DUDE SIGNS.

1. LOOK FOR THESE HIDDEN SYMBOLS ON THE PAGES OF **DUDE VAULT!** THERE IS A NUMBER ON EACH SYMBOL.

2. WHEN YOU FIND THE SYMBOLS, WRITE THE NUMBERS THAT ARE ON EACH SYMBOL IN THE BOXES BELOW, **IN THE ORDER OF HOW THEY APPEAR IN THE DUDE VAULT! BOOK.**

3. GO TO **THEDUDEBOOK.COM**. CLICK ON THE **DUDE VAULT! CODE.** ENTER YOUR CODE FROM ABOVE TO GET ACCESS TO MORE SIGNS.

SEE IT IN 3D

3D DUDE

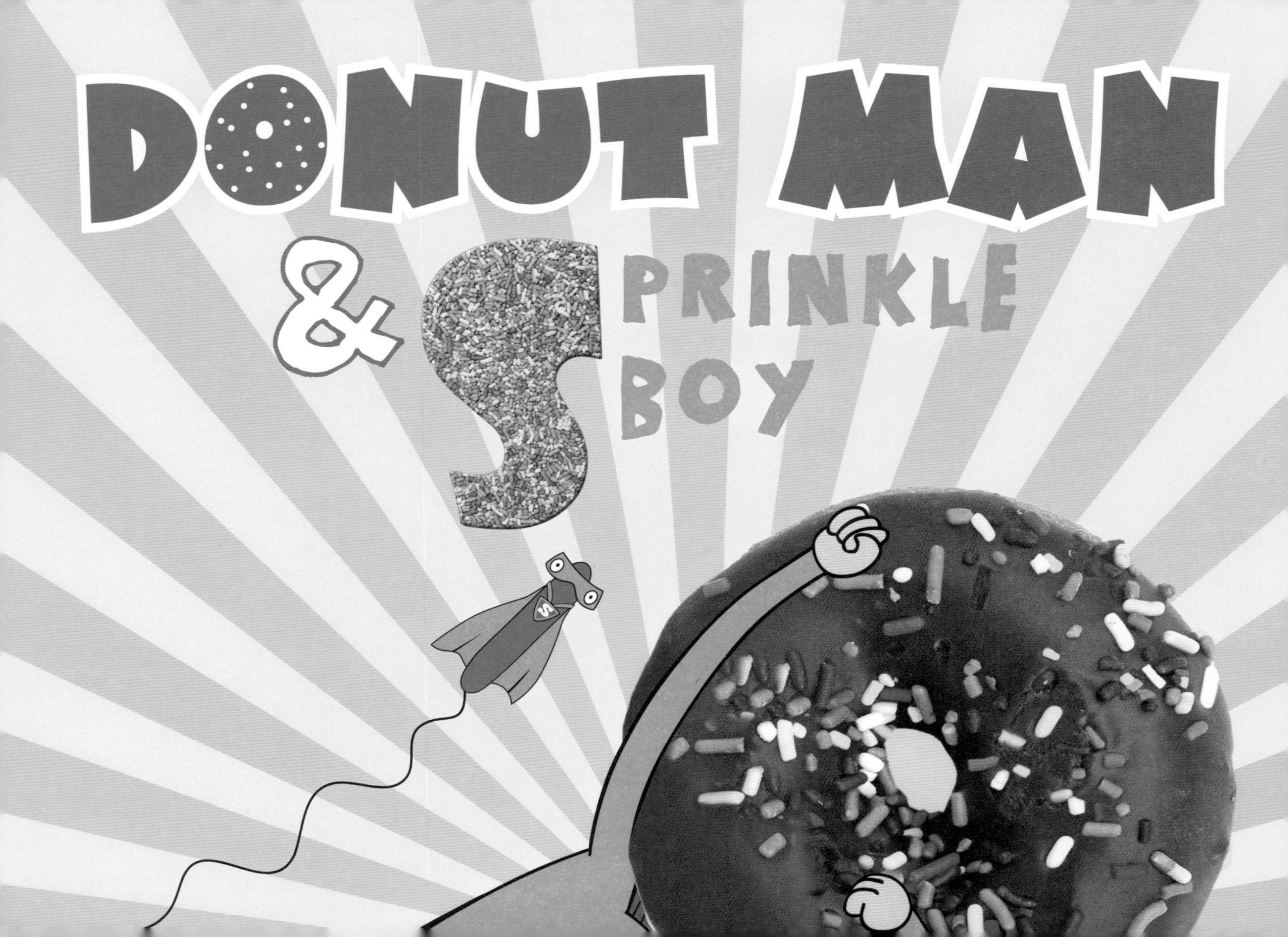
DONUT MAN
& SPRINKLE BOY

WOULD YOU RATHER...

1. be ☐ a pro skateboarder who happens to be a dog
☐ a pro football player who talks like a parrot?

2. have ☐ shape-shifting powers and gorilla feet
☐ bionic hearing and permanent pig tails?

3. ☐ change the litter box for a giant cat
☐ be the pooper scooper for a giant dog?

4. ☐ fly into a black hole and back out on a supersonic go-cart
☐ journey to the Earth's core on a supertectonic pogo stick?

5. be ☐ a badger barber
☐ a boa constrictor masseur?

THAT MEANS YOU'D GIVE ME A MASSAGE

SEE IT IN 3D

3D DUDE

IT'S YOUR PRIVATE FRIDGE IN YOUR BEDROOM! SWEET!

CRAM IT FULL WITH STUFF

YOU
LOVE!
Draw your stash on the shelves.
Lots and lots of meat
Perfect for the dead bugs I find

TOTALLY RIDUNKULOUS GAME CHANG

WRITE NEW, COMPLETELY CRAZY RULES FOR YOUR FAVE SPORT TO PLAY OR WATCH

Name of sport

NEW
and improved
RULES
YOU CAN SCORE POINTS FOR

1. _____

2. _____

3. _____

4. _____

5. _____

YOU'RE IN CHARGE OF TAGGING ALL THE CREATURES IN A MONSTER KENNEL

WITH NAMES, DESCRIPTIONS, & WHAT TO FEED THEIR GUTS

NAME

Creature spits _____ when _____

_____ approaches it. Feeds on _____!

NAME

Six-horned creature can _____.

Feed it _____ & _____ on rainy Thursdays.

NAME

Serpent-like monster _____ every day at midnight.

Shovel _____ into his pie hole every two hours.

NAME

Mammoth mammal tunnels underground & _____ _____. Drinks _____ smoothies.

NAME

Rare pygmy monster uses four arms to _____

_____. Likes to eat _____.

1.
○ A skeleton riding a bike across a tight wire
○ An octopus flipping burgers at a fast food place?

2.
○ Pirates square-dancing at a hoedown
○ Yeti frosting cupcakes in a bakery?

3.
○ Beavers washing windows on a skyscraper
○ Rhinos driving in a monster truck rally?

4.
○ Frankenstein's monster hosting his own TV talk show
○ Zombie performing brain surgery?

5.
○ Chimpanzee working in a crystal chandelier shop
○ Darth Vader instructing a dance class?

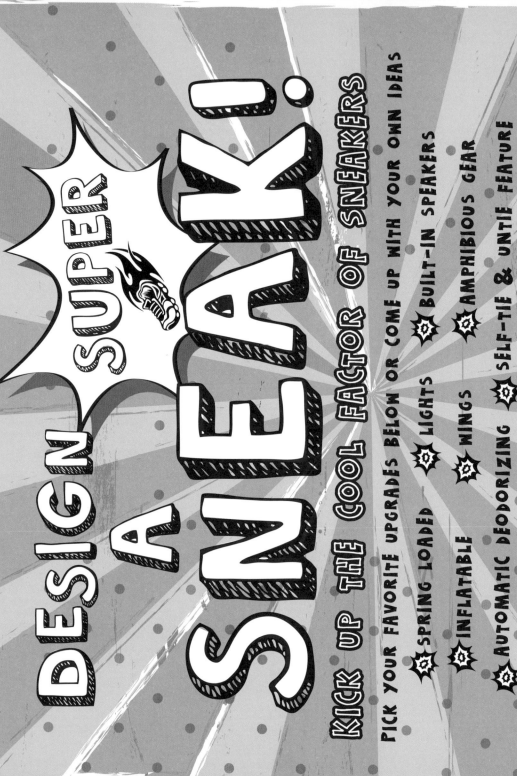

DRAW A LOGO AND THE COOL UPGRADES ON YOUR CREATION

GIVE YOUR SHOES A NAME & DESCRIBE WHAT THEY DO

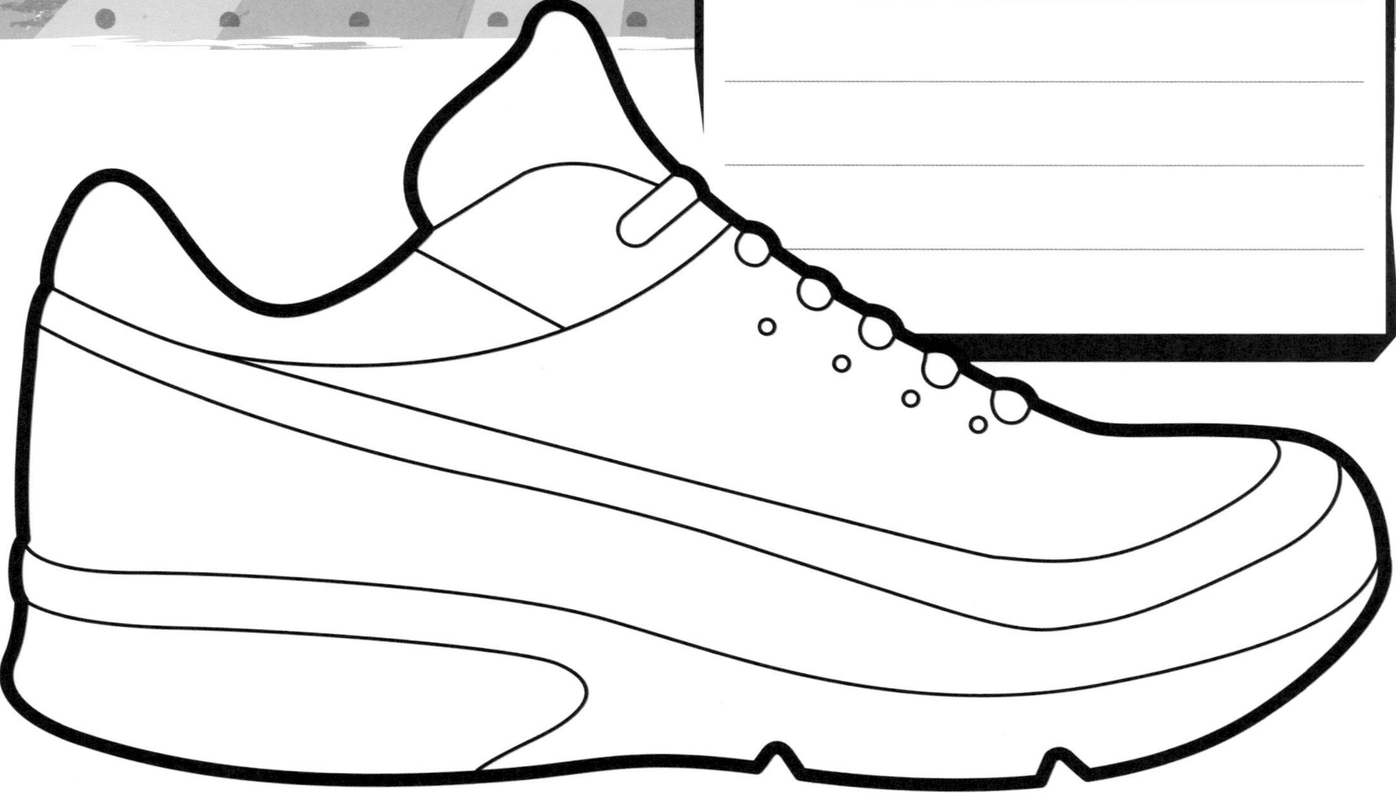

A COMIC BOOK WRITER NEEDS YOUR HELP WITH HIS NEW CHARACTER

A PILE OF DOG POOP GOT CAUGHT IN ALIEN CROSSFIRE.

IT NOW HAS EXTRA-SMELL-ESTRIAL POWERS.

SHOULD IT BE A SUPER ○ HERO ○ VILLAIN? 10

GIVE IT AN AWESOME COMIC BOOK NAME ⬆

WHAT HAPPENS IF...

YOU STEP IN IT? 🍄

↓ YOU TRACK IT IN YOUR HOUSE?

A DOG EATS IT?

YOU'RE IN CHARGE OF AN INSANELY AWESOME RESORT!

SEE IT IN 3D

3D DUDE

COMBINE IDEAS FROM EACH GROUP TO CREATE CRAZY COOL ENTERTAINMENT AND ACTIVITIES

UNDERWATER	JELLO-BASED	DINOSAUR	RAP MUSICAL
UNDERGROUND	RADIOACTIVE	GORILLA	LASER TAG
INTERGALACTIC **+**	MAGICAL **+**	SLUG **+**	GAMING CENTER
SUBTERRANEAN	MUTANT	NINJA	POOL PARTY
AMPHIBIOUS	ELECTRONIC	GIANT CHICKEN	SUB RACING

YOUR OUTRAGEOUS COMBOS

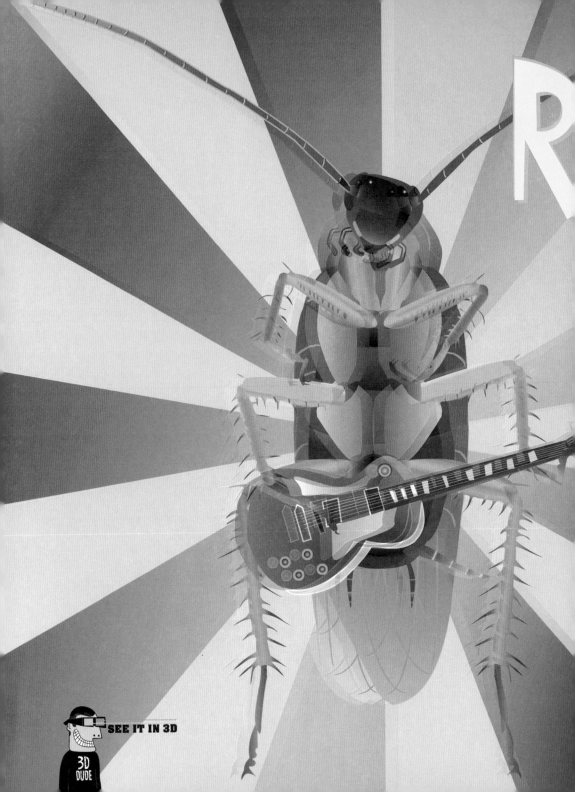

R

CKROACH

IS STARTING A BAND, AND IT NEEDS A COOL NAME.

MASH UP SOME OF THESE WORDS TO COME UP WITH A TOTALLY SICK NAME!

SPECIAL	ROACH	SIX LEGS
MEGA	COCKROACH	GUTS
CREEPY	INSECT	SPLAT
CRAWLING	BUG	SMASH
FLYING	INFESTATION	GARBAGE
KILLER	EXTERMINATOR	KITCHEN FLOOR

BAND NAME IDEAS

_____

_____

_____

_____

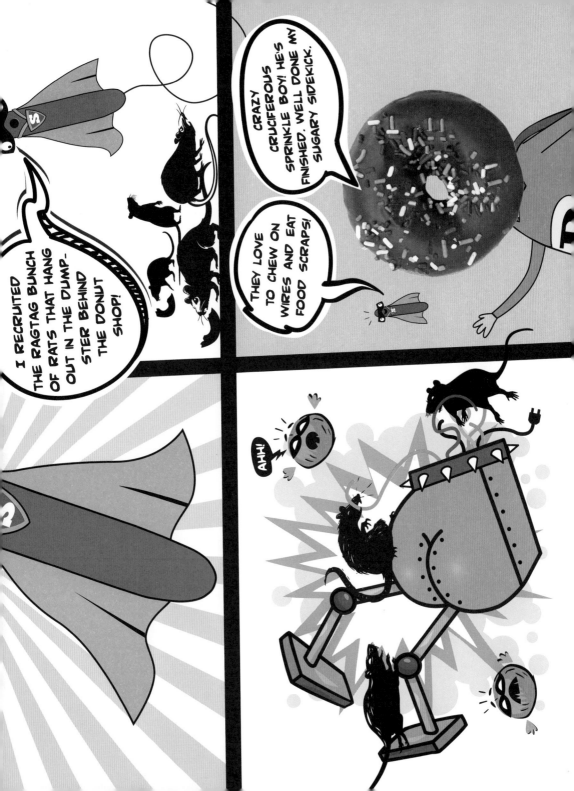

THIS DUDE'S BREATH SMELLS LIKE A

STINK BOMB!

Draw what you think is in his gut.

Dude! This is epically disgusting.

STAIN this shirt with grass, mud, or anything that ruins shirts.

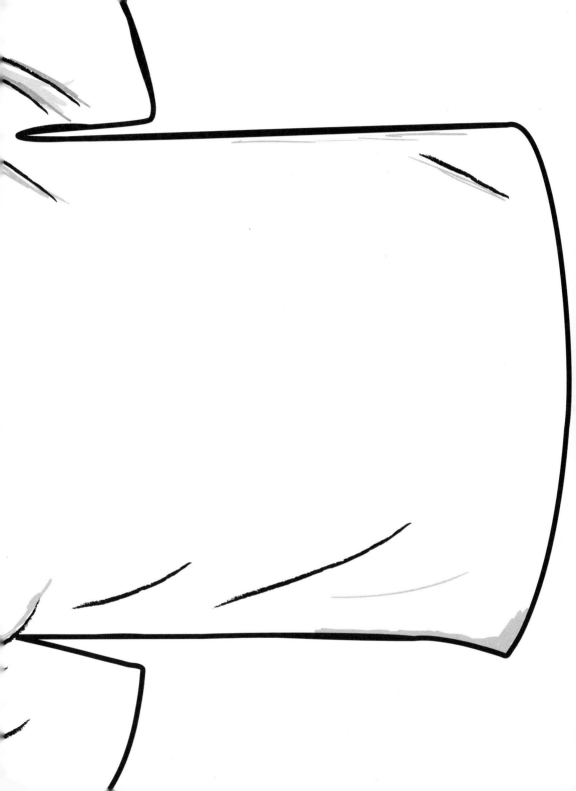

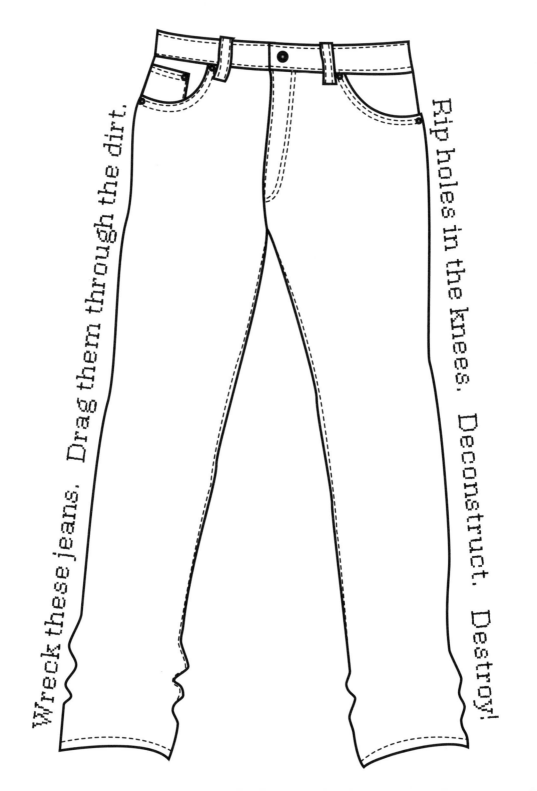

ENTER THE totally MAD LAB HERE

WHAT WILL YOU B[
FR[i]GHTENINGLY FR[

Use some of these parts and your own awesome ideas to create a scary CREEP-ATION

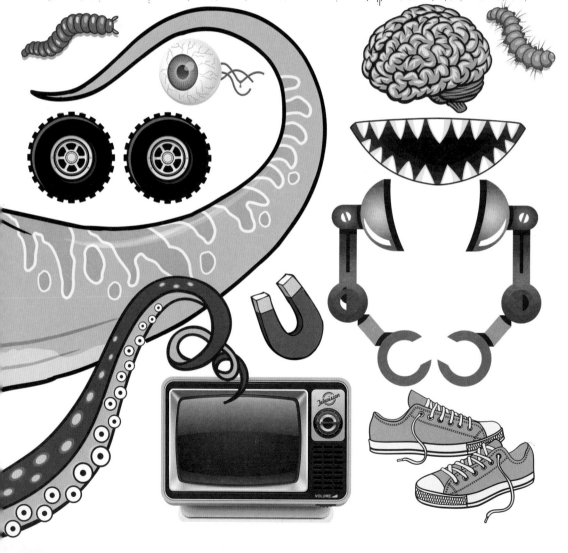

ING TO LIFE IN THE AKY LABORATORY?

Draw it here

Behold the

_____

_____ !

creep-ation name

LAB TECHS ARE WORKING ON A HA-LARIOUS EXPLOSION

Help them mix up the concoction.
What nasty stuff would you combine?

Boogers   Kitty litter
Sewage   Bat breath
Eye gunk   Slime
Moldy cheese   Pond Scum
Dirty underwear   Sweaty socks
Possum poop   Mold
Refried beans   Hairballs
Teeth tartar
Prune pudding

Other _____

SEE IT IN 3D

3D DUDE

Name

Name

Name

GERMS

They go everywhere with you.
They stick to you like glue. Give your posse proper names.

_____
Name

_____
Name

Add faces, arms, legs, and
accessories like
these to them.

_____
Name

WHAT WOULD YOU LOVE TO HAVE THE POWER TO SWITCH ON & OFF?

It would be cool to turn the sun on & off.

Nah, I'd rather turn off all the toilets at school.

LOL WITH AN EVIL VILLAIN

MWAHAHAA!

IS HIS STANDARD LAUGH FOR ALL HIS EVIL DOING. COMBINE SOME OF THE SOUNDS BELOW & CREATE NEW OUTBURSTS 4 HIS DASTARDLY DEEDS.

- ❏ BRAP
- ❏ DOO
- ❏ DWEE
- ❏ WOZ
- ❏ HAW
- ❏ BO
- ❏ LA
- ❏ WEE
- ❏ ZA
- ❏ ARG
- ❏ UH
- ❏ OH
- ❏ EH
- ❏ BLAR
- ❏ OW
- ❏ POO

Write your best one here

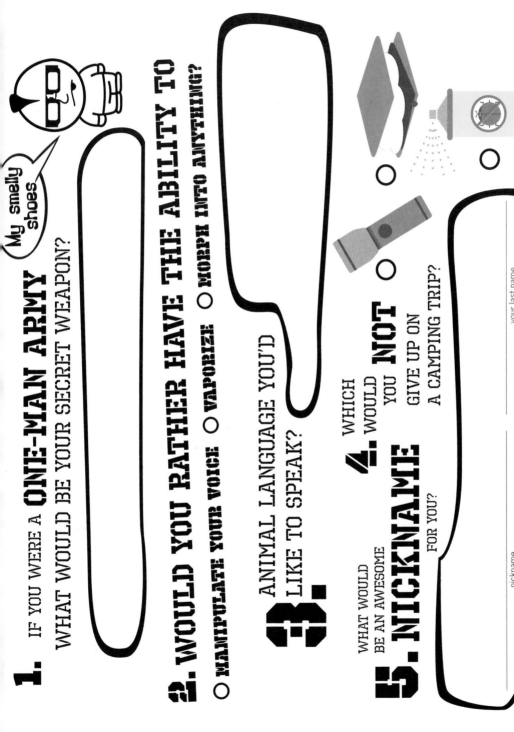

1. IF YOU WERE A **ONE-MAN ARMY**
WHAT WOULD BE YOUR SECRET WEAPON?

My smelly shoes

2. WOULD YOU RATHER HAVE THE ABILITY TO

○ MANIPULATE YOUR VOICE ○ VAPORIZE ○ MORPH INTO ANYTHING?

3. ANIMAL LANGUAGE YOU'D
LIKE TO SPEAK?

4. WHICH
WOULD YOU **NOT** GIVE UP ON
A CAMPING TRIP?

WHAT WOULD
BE AN AWESOME

5. NICKNAME
FOR YOU?

nickname

your last name

MOTO MASH-UP

MIX UP 2 OR MORE CARS.
DESIGN NEW & IMPROVED ULTIMATE RIDES.

Some of your fave cars ↰

LAMBORGHINI   MUSTANG   HUMMER

CHARGER   JAGUAR   PORSCHE

FERRARI   ASTON MARTIN   MASERATI

CORVETTE   ROLLS-ROYCE   VIPER

Mash-up car ideas ↰

DRAW YOUR ULTIMATE COMBO CAR

SHLY STRONG

HE HAS SUPER STRONG STRENGTH, SUPER STRONG BREATH, AND SUPER STRONG STENCH! ANY SITCHES HE CAN HELP YOU WITH?

1

2

3

4

5

SEE IT IN 3D

3D DUDE

1. MOST RIDUNKULOUS THING YOU'VE EVER WORN?

2. DO YOU HAVE A VICTORY DANCE?
•YES •NAH

3. WHAT WOULD BE A DISGUSTING
TOOTHPASTE FLAVOR?

4. WOULD YOU RATHER HAVE A
• POTATO CHIP DIP • DANCE MOVE
• COMET
NAMED AFTER YOU?

5. SOMETHING
YOU'D
LOVE TO VAPORIZE?

HAND OF HORROR

TRACE YOUR FINGERS & TURN THEM INTO GHOULISH CREATURES.

It's the curse of the thumby

Franken-finger

3D DUDE

SEE IT IN 3D

WINTER, SPRING, SUMMER, FALL.

That's all?
COME UP WITH A NEW ONE!

NEW! Season name

When is it? _____ / _____ - _____ / _____
             date   date

What's the weather like?

What do you do this time of year?
Celebrate any holidays?

A Spring-Summer combo. Sprummer.

Slob season. No one makes his bed.

HOW MUCH MONEY WOULD IT TAKE FOR YOU TO...

1. smell your best bro's armpits after p.e. class?

2. chew your toenails?

3. ride on an elevator with a zombie?

4. eat an entire Brussels sprouts - broccoli-tuna loaf?

5. look for a penny at the bottom of a totally full dumpster?

WHAT DOES YOUR ONE-OF-A-KIND

VOLCANO

SEE IT IN 3D

3D DUDE

SPEW WHEN IT ERUPTS?

DRAW IT IN THE SMOKEY CLOUDS.

Giant Boogers!

Chocolate Eclairs

Corn Niblets

DEEP WITHIN THE DUDE VAULT UNIDENTIFIED ARTIFACTS THAT POSSESS SPECIAL POWERS ARE KEPT HIDDEN FROM SOCIETY.

SPECIAL AGENTS NEED YOUR HELP IDENTIFYING THE OBJECTS. FILL OUT THESE TOP SECRET FORMS.

Use your ginormous brain to guess what they are.

NAME _____

CREATED IN _____ _____
                        City   Year

ARTIFACT IS USED FOR _____

_____

_____

NAME _____

CREATED IN _____ _____
                    City   Year

ARTIFACT IS USED FOR _____

_____

_____

NAME _____

FOUND IN _____ _____
                        Place   Year

DESCRIBE ITS ORIGIN _____

_____

_____

THIS IS YOUR TOUR BUS

Now get your tour together.

WHAT'S YOUR GIG?

☐ Band

☐ Cool _sport_ tricks

☐ Pudding cup juggler

☐ Killer sandcastle builder

☐ Long distance spit baller

☐ Terrapin trainer

☐ Other

That's a turtle

NOW GIVE YOUR TOUR A NAME

☐ Spine-tingling ☐ Epic ☐ Awesome ☐ Amazing ☐ Sick ☐ World-changing

THE _____ TOUR!
adjective

gig

Who will go on tour with you?

_____

_____

Which cities, countries, or planets will you visit?

_____

_____

_____

¡WHAT'S FUNNIER?

1.
- TURTLE FRISBEE TOSS TOURNAMENT
- SASQUATCH TAP DANCE PERFORMANCE

2. WOULD YOU RATHER HAVE
- FLAME-THROWING FINGERS
- LASER-SHOOTING NOSTRILS?

SEE IT IN 3D
3D

3. DO YOU HAVE SWAGGER? ○ YES ○ A LITTLE ○ NOT REALLY

4. WHAT'S YOUR BUTT'S FAVORITE T.P.? ○ 2-PLY ○ QUILTED ○ ALOE

5. WOULD YOU RATHER HAVE
○ A CARROT NOSE ○ MUSHROOM EARS ○ CORN KERNEL TEETH?

6. LAST THING THAT
TOUCHED YOUR TASTEBUDS?

7. WHAT'S STUCK BETWEEN YOUR TEETH?

8. WHICH IS MORE AWESOMELY GROSS?
○ SNOT-BASED GLUE ○ NOSE HAIR BRISTLE TOOTH BRUSH?

9. WHAT WOULD BE A HYSTERICAL MIDDLE NAME FOR YOU?

10. WOULD YOU RATHER
HAVE A POCKET-SIZED ○   ○   ○   ?

WHAT DID YOU INHALE THRU YOUR SCHNOZ & INTO YOUR LUNGS TODAY?

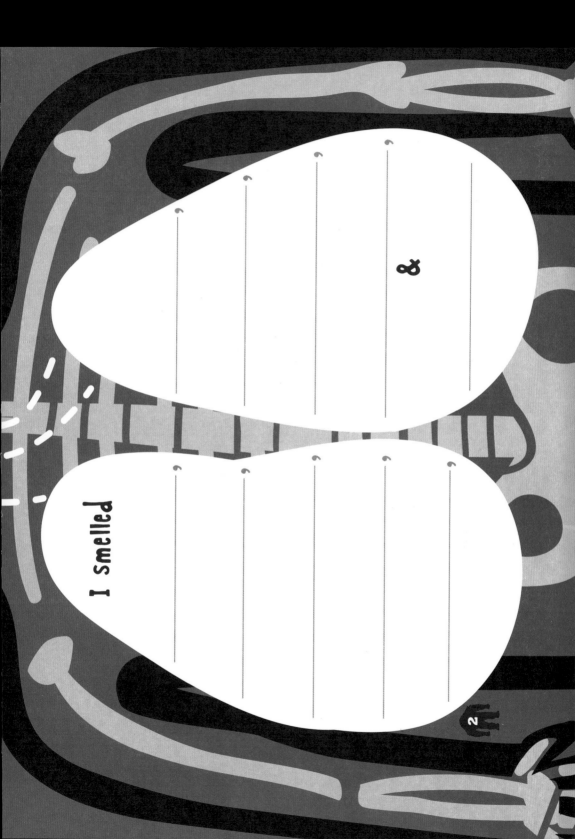

I smelled

&

2

ZOMBiE smoothie!

what other foods would make hilarious living dead creatures?

zombie _____   zombie _____

zombie _____   zombie _____

zombie _____   zombie _____

zombie _____   zombie _____

zombie _____   zombie _____

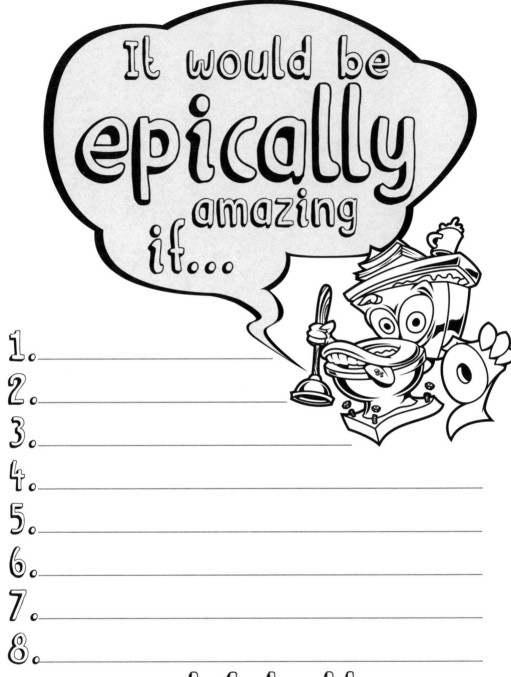

It would be **epically** amazing if...

1. _____
2. _____
3. _____
4. _____
5. _____
6. _____
7. _____
8. _____

could talk.

Post these signs

to keep
non-security-cleared
personnel from
spying
on 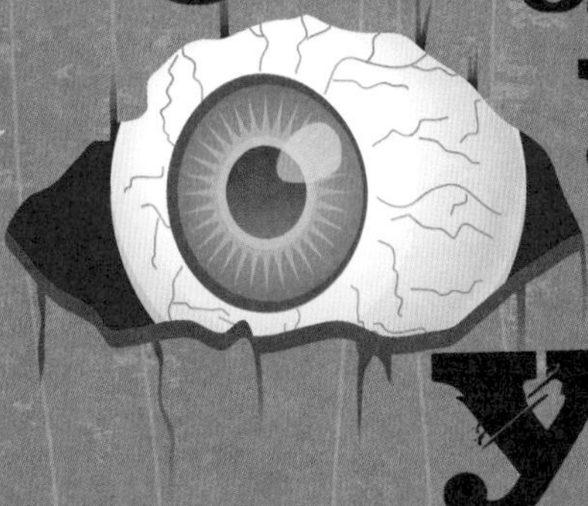
you
when
you
enter
the
DUDE
VAULT!

IF YOU PLAY ME PREPARE TO EAT DEFEAT

PREPARE TO ENTER ANOTHER DIMENSION

NO MATTER WHAT YOU HEAR DO NOT OPEN THIS DOOR

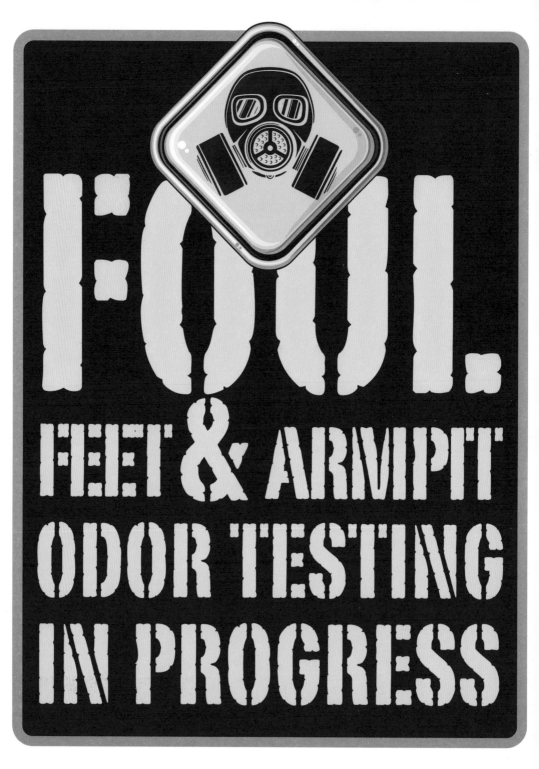

WARNING

NO WEAPONS OR ALIEN TECHNOLOGY BEYOND THIS POINT

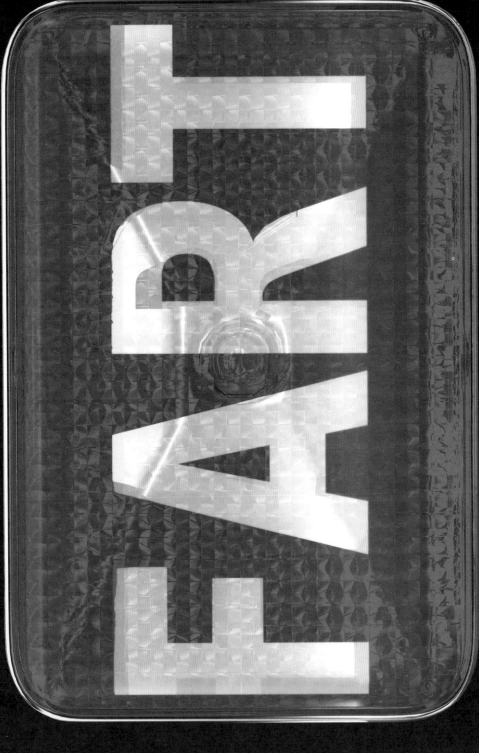

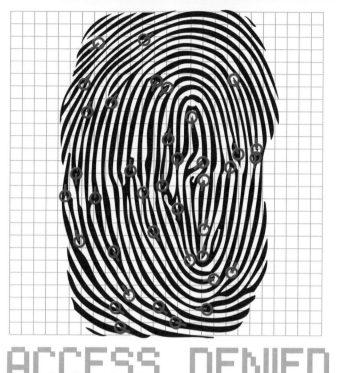

ACCESS DENIED

 PRESS
THUMB
HERE

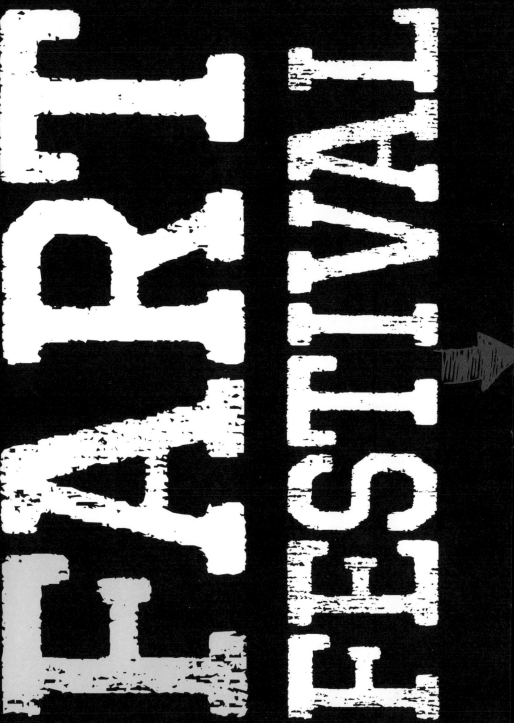

WARNING
OPENING DOOR
ACTIVATES
MONKEY
DUNG
BOMBARDMENT

TODAY'S PASSWORD IS

Hang on door. Write password with chalk. Erase. Repeat.

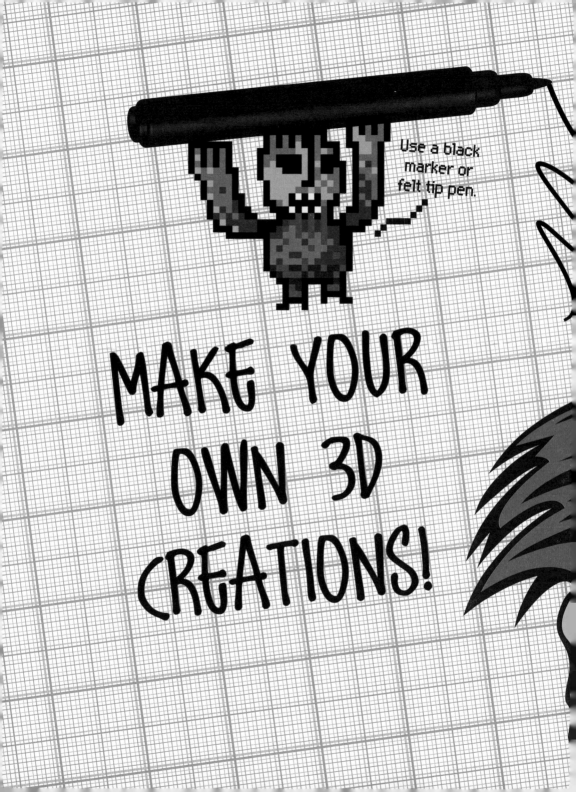

Use a black marker or felt tip pen.

MAKE YOUR OWN 3D CREATIONS!

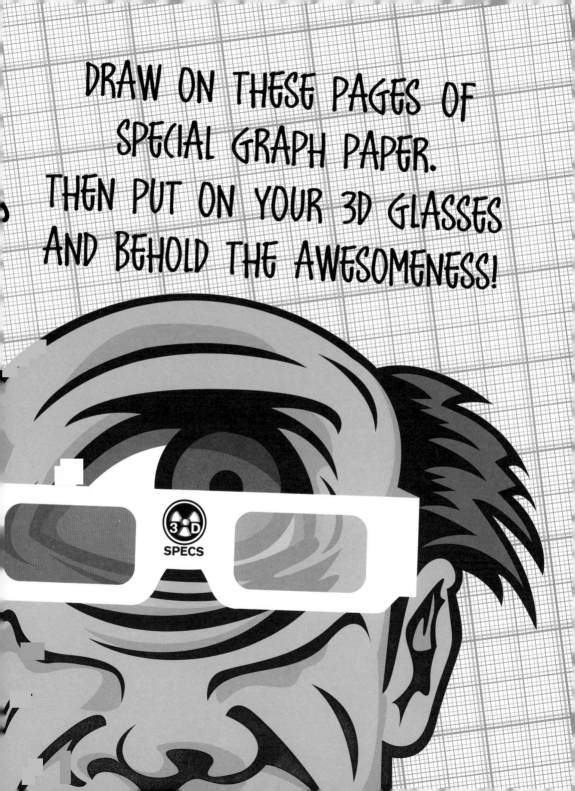

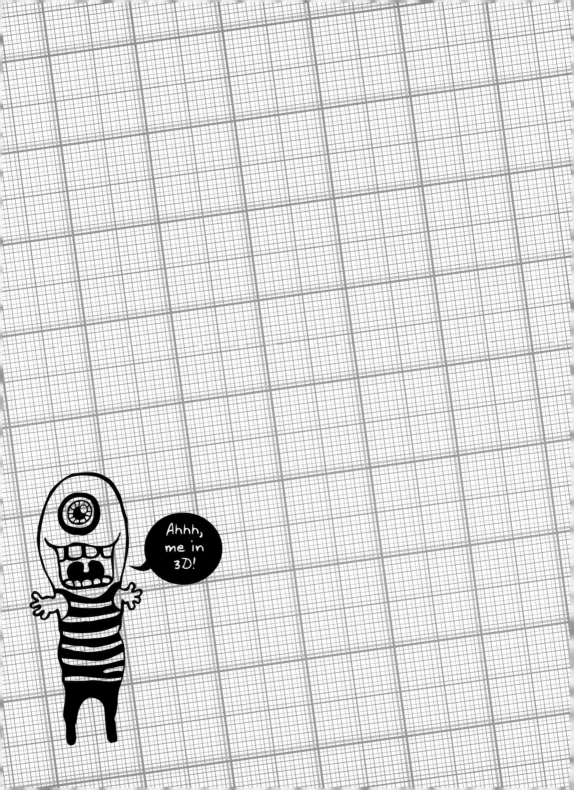

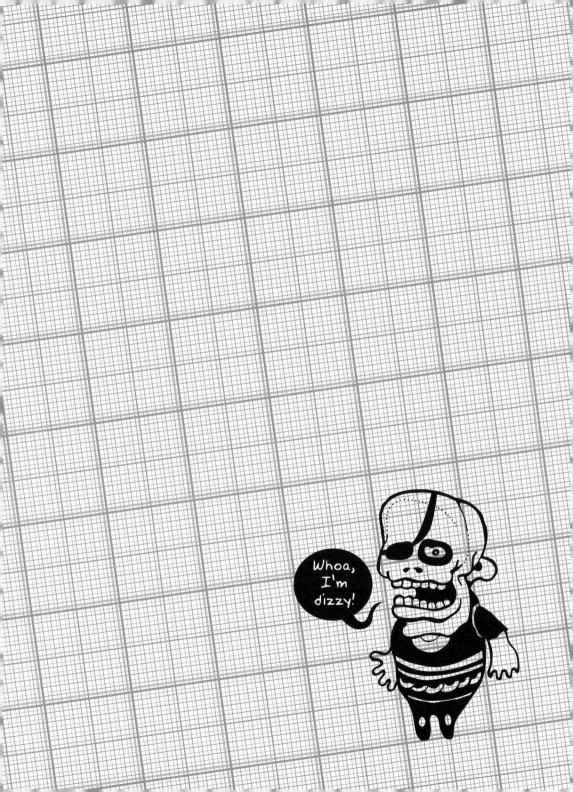

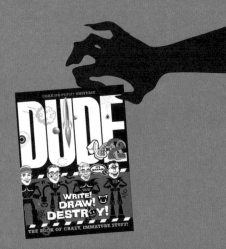

MORE CRAZY DUDE BOOKS ARE WITHIN REACH!

GO TO THEDUDEBOOK.COM TO GET YOUR HANDS ON BOOKS & MORE